The HOLY SPIRIT HIS PRESENCE & WORKS

Decoding the Mystery Behind
the Holy Spirit

GEORGE MFULA

The Holy Spirit, His Presence & Works

Copyright © 2021 by George Mfula

ISBN 978-0-6488810-5-6

Published by Faith Digest Library Media

All rights reserved. No part of this publication may be reproduced, stored in a retrieval system or transmitted in any form or by any means, electronic, mechanical, photocopying, recording or otherwise, without the prior written permission of the copyright owner, with the exception of brief excerpts in magazines, articles, reviews, etc.

For further information or permission, please contact:

Faith Digest Media Library
Rise And Walk Church Inc. SYDNEY AUSTRALIA
Phone: +61. 425-338-781
Email: riseandwalk@hotmail.com
Website: www.riseandwalk.org.au

Text design by: Sriraman Ramachandran
Cover design by: George Mfula
Interior design by: Sriraman Ramachandran

National Library of Australia Cataloguing - in - Publication Data:

Author: Mfula George –
Title: The Holy Spirit, His Presence & Works (pbk)
ISBN 978-0-6488810-5-6
Subjects: Christian Living / Religious Book

Unless otherwise stated, all Scriptures are taken from the New King James Version (The Holy Bible, New King James Version) Copyright © 1982 by Thomas Nelson, Inc. Used by permission. All rights reserved

Contents

Mandate v

Introduction 1

Chapter 1
The Holy Spirit 5

Chapter 2
5 Things About the Holy Spirit 25

Chapter 3
Understanding Spiritual Gifts 43

Chapter 4
Concerning Spiritual Gifts 65

Chapter 5
The Works of the Holy Spirit 101

Chapter 6
Getting Filled with the Spirit 123

Chapter 7
The Fruit of the Holy Spirit..................................143

Final Words of Faith..157

Mandate

God once said to me, "Go! I'm sending you like I sent Moses, my prophet, to liberate my people from all oppressions of the devil through the preaching and teaching of the Word of Faith. Raise the foundations of many generations, prophesy over them and school them into supernatural knowledge, wisdom, and exploits; impart into them my power and wisdom; release them into their glorious and unparalleled destinies."

Introduction

We live at a time in life where understanding of God's divine purpose here on earth is very important. Most often, when people lack spiritual understanding and direction, they lose purpose for living. It is discovering and understanding your purpose in God that empowers your life for greatness. Otherwise, you may get incapacitated in life.

However, it will take the Holy Spirit for you and me to comprehend the major reason of our existence here on earth. Each time you neglect the Holy Spirit in your life, just know that life will become tight or too difficult. You can't succeed in anything you are doing today without the help of the Holy Spirit in Christ Jesus.

The Holy Spirit is outstanding and life giving. We need Him every moment of our lives to encounter the greatness of God. The Holy Spirit is God, He is Jesus here on earth. In fact, Jesus is not here on earth physically, but He exists in us by the Holy Spirit. The voice of the Holy Spirit is the voice of Jesus — you can't separate them!!

There has never been no other time in history we needed the Holy Spirit like now! Of course, the Holy Spirit is eternal — from everlasting to everlasting. However, we are at a time in life where evil is rampart — hence, the need for the Holy Spirit. We need the Holy Spirit to stand strong against all kinds of evil and works of darkness. The Bible says in Matthew 24:24:

Introduction

For false christs and false prophets will rise and show great signs and wonders to deceive, if possible, even the elect."

It will take the Holy Spirit to escape deception of any kind. If you are a true, born-again child of God, you can't afford to live without the Holy Spirit. He is the greatest gift to the body of Christ Jesus. In this book, I will share with you spiritual insights that will revolutionise and empower your life for success and victory in Christ Jesus. There will be an impartation of divine wisdom, knowledge, and understanding. Your spiritual life will never be the same.

I pray as you press on seeking the face of God, you will experience the goodness of God. You will encounter the *Omnipotent* Father of mercy and grace. Your spiritual eyes will open up, and you will see the glory of God. You will also experience total transformation and empowerment in Christ Jesus.

CHAPTER 1

The Holy Spirit

In the beginning God created the heavens and the earth. The earth was without form, and void; and darkness *was* on the face of the deep. And the Spirit of God was hovering over the face of the waters.

Genesis 1:1-2

The Holy Spirit is God

Genesis 1:2

The earth was without form, and void; and darkness *was* on the face of the deep. And the Spirit of God was hovering over the face of the waters.

In the above Scripture, the Bible says, ***"And the Spirit of God was hovering over the face of the water."*** The Hebrew word for the Spirit of God in Genesis 1:2 is "Ruach Elohim," which means "Holy Spirit Creator." Yet, we all know that it was God and Jesus who created everything. How? By the Holy Spirit! The Hebrew word for the Holy Spirit is "Ruach Hakodesh." Jesus, our Lord, who is God, made everything by the Holy Spirit.

John 1:1-3 (AMP)

In the beginning [before all time] was the Word (Christ), and the Word was with God, and the Word was God Himself. He was [continually existing] in the beginning [co-eternally] with God. All things were made *and* came into existence through Him; and without Him not even one thing was made that has come into being.

Jesus, who is God, made all things, including you and me, by the Holy Spirit.

Job 33:4 (AMP)

The Spirit of God has made me, And the breath of the Almighty gives me life [which inspires me].

The Holy Spirit is God Himself—who is also Jesus Christ they co-exist as one eternal God. We sometimes refer the Holy Spirit to the "Spirit of Christ." That is a triune Godhead—three entities in one! God the Father, God the Son and God the Holy Spirit. You can not separate them from each other because they exist as one divine entity.

One time in the Old-Testament, God saw that the wickedness of man was great on the earth. Every imagination of the thoughts of his heart was only evil. Then, it repented Him to have made man on the earth. It grieved His Spirit so much that He ended up destroying the entire earth with the flood. Where God is Jesus is and where God is the Holy is and where the Holy Spirit is, both God and Jesus are.

Genesis 6:1-3

Now it came to pass, when men began to multiply on the face of the earth, and daughters were born to them, that the sons of God saw the daughters of men, that they *were* beautiful; and they took wives for themselves of all whom they chose. And the Lord said, "My Spirit shall not strive with man forever, for he *is* indeed flesh; yet his days shall be one hundred and twenty years."

In the above Scripture, I would love you to note the phrase *"My Spirit shall not strive with man forever, for he is indeed flesh; yet his days shall be one hundred and twenty years."* The word "Spirit" in the preceding sentence stands for the Holy Spirit, who is also God. Throughout the Word of God, you discover God is His Spirit. Whatever God the Father does, God the Spirit and God the Son have also done it. They coexist as one divine entity.

Many years ago, probably in 2006, I prayed for one young man who was bound by the spirit of pornography. In ministering to him, he shared with me his thoughts and understanding concerning the Holy Spirit. He did not think the Holy Spirit was God. That was the teaching he received from his Church. Look, misinterpretation of God's Word will always lead to satanic oppression or bondage.

Sad to say, the young man did not regard the Holy Spirit as God—not at all. If you just take the Holy Spirit as a wind, fire, or a breeze, you will miss out on your life and destiny. The Holy Spirit is God and whatever God does, He does it by the Holy Spirit. Whatever Jesus does, He does it by the Holy Spirit. The Holy Spirit is God Himself! I pray you won't miss out on the Holy Spirit because you luck spiritual understanding.

Isaiah 44:3-4

For I will pour out water on him who is thirsty, And streams on the dry ground; I will pour out My Spirit on your offspring And My blessing on your descendants.

Failure to believe that the Holy Spirit is God leads to bondage. There is nothing the Holy Spirit can do about it—you have reduced Him to something else. When you regard someone as a medical doctor, you will provide room for him or her to operate in your life as a medical doctor. Yes, that is the way it is and it can't be changed at all.

In the same manner, if you regard the Holy Spirit as God, you will give Him room to operate in your life as God. However, if you don't give Him room in your life as God, He won't operate in your life as God. Why? That is because you have reduced him to something else He isn't. If you don't acknowledge the Holy Spirit as God, just know He won't change your life. The Holy Spirit is God, and that is forever settled in Heaven.

Matthew 28:18-20

And Jesus came and spoke to them, saying, "All authority has been given to Me in heaven and on earth. Go therefore and make disciples of all the nations, baptizing them in the name of the Father and of the Son and of the Holy Spirit, teaching them to observe all things that I have commanded you; and lo, I am with you always, *even* to the end of the age." Amen.

God the Father, God the Son and God the Holy Spirit co-exist as one eternal God, but have different functionalities. This makes them superb!

1 John 5:5-7

Who is he who overcomes the world, but he who believes that Jesus is the Son of God? This is He who came by water and blood–Jesus Christ; not only by water, but by water and blood. And it is the Spirit who bears witness, because the Spirit is truth. For there are three that bear witness in heaven: the Father, the Word, and the Holy Spirit; and these three are one.

You can't separate the Holy Spirit from God the Father, and God the Son. They are all one yet have different functionalities. A good example is when you buy any kind of coffee. It has three elements: coffee, sugar and milk. They all have different functions — yet they give one taste we call "nice coffee." The function of sugar differs from that of coffee and milk, yet they are all working together. They co-exist as coffee, yet three in one.

The Spirit of Christ

1 Peter 1:10-11

Of this salvation the prophets have inquired and searched carefully, who prophesied of the grace *that would come* to you, searching what, or what manner of time, the Spirit of Christ who was in them was indicating when He testified beforehand the sufferings of Christ and the glories that would follow.

The Spirit of Christ is basically the Holy Spirit. Without doubt, we are blessed to have received the Spirit of Christ, who is also the Holy Spirit. Once again, I would love you to understand that God the Father, God the Son and God the Spirit may have different functionalities, yet they coexist as one divine entity.

Romans 8:8-9

So then, those who are in the flesh cannot please God. But you are not in the flesh but in the Spirit, if indeed the Spirit of God dwells in you. Now if anyone does not have the Spirit of Christ, he is not His.

I know that every true child of God has the Spirit of Christ in them, who is also the Holy Spirit. You can't separate Jesus from God, and the Holy Spirit from Jesus—they are three in one, but distinct entities. That is why they are called the "Triune Godhead." Once you have this understanding, your life won't be the same again.

Now, for Jesus to help His disciples understand that God and Him were the same, Jesus said to Philip the disciple, He who has seen me has seen the Father. Of course, when you see the Holy Spirit, you have seen Jesus and God. Then, when you see Jesus, you have also seen God the Father and God the Holy Spirit. Why? That is because Jesus looks exactly like the Father does and they coexist as one divine entity.

John 14:8-9

Philip said to Him, "Lord, show us the Father, and it is sufficient for us." Jesus said to him, "Have I been with you so long, and yet you have not known Me, Philip? He who has seen Me has seen the Father; so how can you say, 'Show us the Father'?

The Spirit of Christ in you is the Holy Spirit, who is also the mark of ownership that you belong to God. The moment Jesus comes into your life, the Holy Spirit also comes into your life. Yes, the Holy Spirit becomes the guarantee that we are God's property or that we belong to God.

Ephesians 4:30

And do not grieve the Holy Spirit of God, by whom you were sealed for the day of redemption.

Ephesians 1:13-14

In Him you also *trusted,* after you heard the word of truth, the gospel of your salvation; in whom also, having believed, you were sealed with the Holy Spirit of promise, who is the guarantee of our inheritance until the redemption of the purchased possession, to the praise of His glory.

I pray you will start operating in the higher dimensions of the Holy Spirit. May the Spirit of Christ, who is also the Holy Spirit, take over your life. In fact, the Holy Spirit is Jesus here on earth! When Jesus comes into your life, He exists in you by the Holy Spirit. Besides, the Holy Spirit is here on earth to reveal and glorify the person of Jesus Christ.

John 16:12-15

"I still have many things to say to you, but you cannot bear *them* now. However, when He, the Spirit of truth, has come, He will guide you into all truth; for He will not speak on His own *authority,* but whatever He hears He will speak; and He will tell you things to come. He will glorify Me, for He will take of what is Mine and declare *it* to you. All things that the Father has are Mine. Therefore I said that He will take of Mine and declare *it* to you.

The Holy Spirit will glorify Jesus in your life to dimensions you have never seen.

1 Corinthians 2:9-11

But as it is written: "Eye has not seen, nor ear heard, Nor have entered into the heart of man The things which God has prepared for those who love Him." But God has revealed them to us through His Spirit. For the Spirit searches all things, yes, the deep things of God. For what man knows the things of a man except the spirit of the man which is in him? Even so no one knows the things of God except the Spirit of God.

I pray that the Holy Spirit will be real in your life, in Jesus' name.

The Spirit of Grace

The Holy Spirit is also the *Spirit of grace*. He is the one who enforces the grace of God in our lives.

Hebrews 10:29-30

Of how much worse punishment, do you suppose, will he be thought worthy who has trampled the Son of God underfoot and counted the blood of the covenant by which he was sanctified a common thing, and insulted the Spirit of grace? For we know Him who said, "Vengeance is Mine, I will repay," says the Lord. And again, "The Lord will judge His people."

In the Scripture above, I would love you to note the phrase *"and insulted the Spirit of grace."* Can you notice they capitalized the letter S in the word Spirit, referring to the Spirit of God or the Holy Spirit? The Holy Spirit is the Spirit of grace. For example, if you have fallen into sin, then you call upon Jesus to forgive you of your sins. The Holy Spirit is the one that makes the grace of God real to you—yes, He does!

Apart from that, no one today can make it in life without the Spirit of grace who is also the Holy Spirit. The Holy Spirit has an integral part in our lives and salvation. Many Christians don't understand that the Holy Spirit is the one behind our spirituality. Besides, no one can even say Jesus Christ is Lord except by the Holy Spirit.

1 Corinthians 12:3

Therefore I make known to you that no one speaking by the Spirit of God calls Jesus accursed, and no one can say that Jesus is Lord except by the Holy Spirit.

Everyone needs the grace of God! No one can find salvation without the Spirit of grace. The Bible says in John 1:17, *"For the law was given through Moses, but grace and truth came through Jesus Christ."* Hence, sinners, prostitutes, or murderers today can find forgiveness in Christ Jesus. Why? This is because of the unfailing love and grace of God at work in our lives.

Hebrews 4:16

Let us therefore come boldly to the throne of grace, that we may obtain mercy and find grace to help in time of need.

It doesn't matter how wicked your life is today, the Spirit of grace is there to save you from sin. Now, without the Spirit of grace not one person can receive Jesus in their lives. It is the Spirit of grace that brings people to the cross for repentance and forgiveness. Once again, salvation is impossible without the Spirit of grace or the Holy Spirit.

It is the Holy Spirit who convicts people of sin and then reveals the grace of God to them. Apart from that, it is at the revelation of God's grace that people find Jesus. You may preach the Word of God, but if the grace of God doesn't get revealed to them, they will remain bound in sin, with no sense of conviction at all.

Unless people find the grace of God, they can't get saved. Also, just because the grace of God is there does not mean people will come to Jesus. No! It will take the Spirit of grace to make the essence of salvation real to them. Only then can you see them come to Jesus in repentance. Anyone who found the grace of God never remained the same.

Genesis 6:5-8

> Then the Lord saw that the wickedness of man *was* great in the earth, and *that* every intent of the thoughts of his heart *was* only evil continually. And the Lord was sorry that He had made man on the earth, and He was grieved in His heart. So the Lord said, "I will destroy man whom I have created from the face of the earth, both man and beast, creeping thing and birds of the air, for I am sor-

ry that I have made them." But Noah found grace in the eyes of the Lord.

It was the grace of God that Noah found and gave him a place in God's redemption. I pray that the Holy Spirit will reveal to you the very grace of God for your rescue in Christ Jesus.

CHAPTER 2

5 Things About the Holy Spirit

"I still have many things to say to you, but you cannot bear *them* now. However, when He, the Spirit of truth, has come, He will guide you into all truth; for He will not speak on His own *authority,* but whatever He hears He will speak; and He will tell you things to come. He will glorify Me, for He will take of what is Mine and declare *it* to you. All things that the Father has are Mine. Therefore I said that He will take of Mine and declare *it* to you.

John 16:12-15

(1). He is a Person

John 15:26 (AMP)

"But when the Helper (Comforter, Advocate, Intercessor–Counselor, Strengthener, Standby) comes, whom I will send to you from the Father, *that is* the Spirit of Truth who comes from the Father, He will testify *and* bear witness about Me.

The Holy Spirit is not a wind, a breeze, or a force. Instead, He is a divine Spirit with a personality to Himself. When we relate to Him, we can relate with Him in the same way we relate with our fellow human beings, but in a divine way. You can't have a relationship with the Holy Spirit if He was just a wind, a force, or a fire.

Sometimes the Holy Spirit may manifest as wind, but He is not wind. He may also manifest as a breeze, but He is not a breeze. He is God and has a personality to Himself. Of course, He may come into a meeting as a fire or a force, but He is more than that. Hence, we wouldn't have a relationship with Him if He was just an object or a tool. No one speaks to an object, to a fire, to a wind or to a breeze. Not at all!

John 16:13 (AMP)

But when He, the Spirit of Truth, comes, He will guide you into all the truth [full and complete truth]. For He will not speak on His own initiative, but He will speak whatever He hears [from the Father–the message regarding the Son], and He will disclose to you what is to come [in the future].

I pray you will seek a rich relationship with the Holy Spirit as never in Jesus' name.

(2). He Speaks

Acts 13:1-3

Now in the church that was at Antioch there were certain prophets and teachers: Barnabas, Simeon who was called Niger, Lucius of Cyrene, Manaen who had been brought up with Herod the tetrarch, and Saul. As they ministered to the Lord and fasted, the Holy Spirit said, "Now separate to Me Barnabas and Saul for the work to which I have called them." Then, having fasted and prayed, and laid hands on them, they sent *them* away.

Once again, the Holy Spirit speaks! You can have an actual conversation with Him. He is not dumb as a wind or an object. Hence, this brings us back to say if He was a wind or a force or a breeze, how could He speak? It is obvious to say that a wind, or a breeze or a fire can not speak or talk. They don't have the ability or characteristics to do so. They are elements or objects in nature. Unlike the Holy Spirit, who speaks!

Look, the Holy Spirit speaks with a clear, small, still, and sweet voice. In Acts 13:1-5, He spoke to the Apostles of Jesus Christ as they gathered together for prayer and fasting in Antioch. However, if you want to access the voice of the Holy Spirit or to hear what He is saying in your life, you have to be in the Spirit. Many Christians think to hear the Holy Spirit is that easy. No! You have to position yourself in the Spirit.

Revelations 1:10-11

I was in the Spirit on the Lord's Day, and I heard behind me a loud voice, as of a trumpet, saying, "I am the Alpha and the Omega, the First and the Last," and, "What you see, write in a book and send *it* to the seven churches which are in Asia: to Ephesus, to Smyrna, to Pergamos, to Thyatira, to Sardis, to Philadelphia, and to Laodicea."

The voice of the Holy Spirit is the voice of Jesus—it is the voice of God. God doesn't speak just anyhow. Even when He speaks, you have to be in the right realm or dimension. Just like you can tune your radio to the right radio frequency, the same way you can tune your born-gain spirit to the frequency of the Holy Spirit. Otherwise, you can't hear the Holy Spirit without tuning your spirit-man by God's Word and prayer.

Developing your born-again human spirit is one way to position yourself to hear from God. There are several ways to develop your born-again human spirit, namely: (1). Reading and studying God's Word (2). Prayer and fasting (3). Praise and Worship (4). Waiting upon the Lord in silence. People who don't hear from the Holy Spirit will always get stranded in life.

I believe what the Holy Spirit speaks to you about is the key to a life of transformation, victory, favour, and progress. The beauty of your entire future is in the voice of God — the voice of the Holy Spirit. Many people, even Christians, cry to God for miracles, breakthroughs, signs, and wonders. Well, sometimes God's answer comes via the voice of the Holy Spirit, which you have to hear, believe, and act upon in faith.

Psalm 29:3-4

The voice of the Lord *is* over the waters; The God of glory thunders; The Lord *is* over many waters. The voice of the Lord *is* powerful; The voice of the Lord *is* full of majesty.

Acts 11:12

Then the Spirit told me to go with them, doubting nothing. Moreover these six brethren accompanied me, and we entered the man's house.

Acts 8:27-29

So he arose and went. And behold, a man of Ethiopia, a eunuch of great authority under Candace the queen of the Ethiopians, who had charge of all her treasury, and had come to Jerusalem to worship, was returning. And sitting in his chariot, he was reading Isaiah the prophet. Then the Spirit said to Philip, "Go near and overtake this chariot."

You can't change levels of progress in your life if you can't hear the Holy Spirit. I pray that your relationship with the Holy Spirit will change levels in Jesus' name. Neglecting the Holy Spirit is crushing your own destiny without knowing. The greatest investment you can ever do in your life is to develop your born-again human spirit on how to hear the voice of the Holy Spirit in Christ Jesus.

(3). He Hears

2 Chronicles 7:14

If My people who are called by My name will humble themselves, and pray and seek My face, and turn from their wicked ways, then I will hear from heaven, and will forgive their sin and heal their land.

What the above Scripture implies is that when you pray, God will hear your prayers by His Spirit. Without doubt, the Holy Spirit gets involved with our prayers to have them answered. Each time we open our mouth to pray, the Spirit of the Sovereign Lord hears us. However, we don't know how to pray by ourselves—yes; we don't! It is the Holy Spirit who helps us to pray according to the will of God in Christ Jesus.

Romans 8:26-27

Likewise the Spirit also helps in our weaknesses. For we do not know what we should pray for as we ought, but the Spirit Himself makes intercession for us with groanings which cannot be uttered. Now He who searches the hearts knows what the mind of the Spirit is, because He makes intercession for the saints according to the will of God.

People think prayer is that easy, even to have your prayers answered. If you don't engage the Holy Spirit with your prayers, God may not hear you. As humans, we don't know how to pray. However, when we engage the Holy Spirit, answers to our prayers will come. Sometimes, you may think you have prayed the right way by looking at your grammar or voice projection. Of course that is good, but doesn't count at all.

Cain and Abel in the book of Genesis 4:1-16 brought offerings to the Lord, which was a type of prayer. God listened to Abel's prayers or offering, but not Cain's. Why?

It is the same reason we need the Holy Spirit today to enable us to pray effectively. No doubt about it, you can pray even do some fasting, but without the Holy Spirit empowering your prayers, nothing may come to pass. Just be careful in life!!

Just because you open your mouth and pray, is not a guarantee that God has heard your prayers. No! It will take the Holy Spirit for God to hear your prayers. Besides, the Holy Spirit can only hear us when we pray in humility and acknowledgement of His person in our lives. I encourage you to develop a rich relationship with the Holy Spirit, and your life will never be the same.

(4) He Can Get Grieved

Ephesians 4:30

And do not grieve the Holy Spirit of God [but seek to please Him], by whom you were sealed *and* marked [branded as God's

own] for the day of redemption [the final deliverance from the consequences of sin].

Many times, the thing that causes the Holy Spirit to get grieved is when we walk in disobedience to His instructions and guidance. Why? This is because He loves us so very much—He wants the best for us. However, He doesn't grieve like someone in "intense grief" or who has lost something precious. No! He grieves regarding our relationship with God, especially when we walk away from God in disobedience.

The Holy Spirit loves us, hence, He wants us to walk in God's divine blessings. However, walking away from God will always grieve the Holy Spirit beyond measure. Once again, the Holy Spirit doesn't want you and me to miss Heaven because of our disobedience. He is a Holy and loving Spirit. In addition, He doesn't want us to walk in defeat, misery or hopelessness here on earth.

I believe sin in our lives grieves the Holy Spirit the most. That is why the Bible says, *"Do not grieve the Holy Spirit."* We can't live the way we want and expect the Holy Spirit to do great things in our midst. No! The first thing we must always desire and look forward to is to please the Holy Spirit. When we please the Holy Spirit, we have also pleased God and our Lord Jesus Christ. Grieving the Holy Spirit is very dangerous!

Ephesians 4:30-32

And do not grieve the Holy Spirit of God, by whom you were sealed for the day of redemption. Let all bitterness, wrath, anger, clamor, and evil speaking be put away from you, with all malice. And be kind to one another, tenderhearted, forgiving one another, even as God in Christ forgave you.

The Holy Spirit loves you, and He wants the best for your life. Thus, I encourage you to forsake all kinds of evil and unrighteousness.

(5). He Can Get Quenched

1 Thessalonians 5:19

Do not quench [subdue, or be unresponsive to the working and guidance of] the [Holy] Spirit.

What is the dictionary meaning of the word "quench?" Well, it means: *"to put out, to extinguish, to put out the light or fire or to cool down something, such as heated metal by immersion as in oil or water."* I have seen how when you put a hot substance in cold water, it gets cooled down. We call that cooling as *quenching*.

Likewise, the Holy Spirit in your life can get quenched—put out or extinguished. When that happens, you are neither hot nor cold. Then you come to a place where you don't even know where you belong as a child of God. You are a Christian, but you can still visit strip clubs or worldly entertainments. That is because you have lost the fire of the Holy Spirit.

You can't carry the fire of the Holy Spirit and still find yourself in places that do not glorify Jesus. No! I believe it is time you rekindled the lost fire of the Holy Spirit in your life. Many believers, even Christians, have lost the fire of the Holy Spirit. The Holy Spirit gets grieved each time we wilfully allow evil into our lives. Apart from that, He also gets quenched—He is there in your life, but doing nothing—no effects!

In some churches, the Holy Spirit fire is quenched. It is no longer there! We have put out that fire by allowing the flesh and its desires to be at work. It is sad to say, some churches have closed down today. Why? I believe the Holy Spirit left those churches a long time ago. Each time we introduce our own worship or ideas to what is sacred, we quench the Holy Spirit. He is holy and can't stay where sin is.

Once again, the number one thing that quenches the Holy Spirit out of our lives is sin. Especially, disobedience to God's voice and Word. People walking in unforgiveness, falsehood, pride, jealousy, envy, anger, bitterness and every other carnal thing will quench the fire of the Holy Spirit. Hence, we need to stay away from sin or anything that will quench the fire of the Holy Spirit. We need urgent help from God!

Many years ago, I read something powerful from Kenneth E. Hagin's book. He said many times when praying for people in his meetings, he would sense the Holy Spirit leave him. Why? It was because of distractions within the building. Why would the

Holy Spirit leave in the first place? It is because He gets grieved or quenched where there are distractions in a meeting—hence departing from your midst.

Judges 16:18-20

Then Delilah realized that he had told her everything in his heart, so she sent and called for the Philistine lords, saying, "Come up this once, because he has told me everything in his heart." Then the Philistine lords came up to her and brought the money [they had promised] in their hands. She made Samson sleep on her knees, and she called a man and had him shave off the seven braids of his head. Then she began to abuse Samson, and his strength left him. She said, "The Philistines are upon you, Samson!" And he awoke from his sleep and said, "I will go out as I have time after time and shake myself free." For Samson did not know that the Lord had departed from him.

My prayer is that you will develop a rich relationship with the Holy Spirit. Jesus wants to invade your life with His goodness by the power of the Holy Spirit. Will you create room for Him? I pray God bless you as you press into seeking the Holy Spirit, His presence and works.

CHAPTER 3

Understanding Spiritual Gifts

Now concerning spiritual *gifts*, brethren, I do not want you to be ignorant: You know that you were Gentiles, carried away to these dumb idols, however you were led. Therefore I make known to you that no one speaking by the Spirit of God calls Jesus accursed, and no one can say that Jesus is Lord except by the Holy Spirit.

1 Corinthians Ch: 12:1-3

What are Spiritual Gifts?

Apostle Paul once said:

Romans 1:11

For I long to see you, that I may impart to you some spiritual gift, so that you may be established.

Just by the term spiritual gifts, something will tell you that these are spiritual endowments. You don't pay for them — they get apportioned to you as the Spirit of God wills. Every child of God today needs spiritual gifts, either for ministry or spiritual growth. Without doubt, God designed spiritual gifts for the establishment of the saints or Church. Spiritual gifts will always establish the lives and destinies of people in no time.

Spiritual gifts are there to establish the lives and destinies of people, even the lost. I have seen people who lost it all in life get transformed after encountering the God of spiritual gifts. Sometimes, in order to restore destinies of people hooked on drugs or pornography, God will send a man or woman of God with diverse spiritual gift into their lives.

Besides, you also discover that people may sometimes live without purpose for many reasons. Then, suddenly, God sends a man or woman of God with spiritual gifts to open up a church in that location. He will then call people to come and attend church services. Apart from that, people will get healed, delivered, restored, enlightened and empowered to live for Jesus. That is what spiritual gifts can do!

The man or woman of God is a spiritual gift to that community or generation. Eventually, you will find out that the lives and destinies of people in that locality get transformed and established. Those who were on drugs quit and discover their glorious purpose in Christ Jesus. Then, the marriages of those who were on the verge of divorce get mended and restored.

Then, young men or women get empowered in life to pursue their high school or university studies in a grand style. That is what spiritual gifts can do! In the end, the people that God so loves get restored and blessed beyond measure. Hence, all we need today is to understand the power of spiritual gifts in Christ Jesus. Sorry to say, spiritual gifts are not there for selfish gains, but to bring glory and honour to God.

Spiritual gifts are for delivering God's people or lost souls from destruction. Hence, if you have gifts from God in any area, don't take them for granted. One gift of a child of God can preserve a generation from destruction. If God has gifted you to sing for Him, don't take that for granted. If God has endowed upon you the gift to preach, don't take that for granted. Whatever gift of God you have matters to this generation.

Luke 4:18-20

"The Spirit of the Lord *is* upon Me, Because He has anointed Me To preach the gospel to *the* poor; He has sent Me to heal the brokenhearted, To proclaim liberty to *the* captives And recovery of sight to *the* blind, *To* set at liberty those who are oppressed; To proclaim the acceptable year of the Lord." Then He closed the book, and gave *it* back to the attendant and sat down. And the eyes of all who were in the synagogue were fixed on Him.

Spiritual gifts are for delivering lost souls or children of God from destruction. Hence, if you have gifts from God in any area, don't take them for granted. One gift of a child of God can transform and preserve a generation from destruction or decadence.

If God has gifted you to sing for Him, don't take that for granted. If God has endowed upon you the gift to pray for the sick, don't take that for granted. Whatever gift you have from God matters to this generation.

Many years ago, the Lord revealed to me the matchless value of the gifts He has given you and I. There may be millions of people who are waiting for the same spiritual gifts God has given you. What you do with those gifts will determine the destination of those people. What are you going to say to God on the day of judgement? Just make sure you put those spiritual gifts God has endowed upon your life to work.

Matthew 25:24-25

Then he who had received the one talent came and said, 'Lord, I knew you to be a hard man, reaping where you have not sown, and gathering where you have not scattered seed. And I was afraid, and went and hid your talent in the ground. Look, *there* you have *what is* yours.'

It is your responsibility to put your spiritual gifts to work—do not wait for your pastor!

Matthew 25:26-28

"But his lord answered and said to him, 'You wicked and lazy servant, you knew that I reap where I have not sown, and gather where I have not scattered seed. So you ought to have deposited my money with the bankers, and at my coming I would have received back my own with interest. So take the talent from him, and give *it* to him who has ten talents.

The very reason that God has gifted you is enough to say He believes in you. The Almighty God gives the gifts, then our Lord Jesus Christ administers them to us by the Holy Spirit. Without doubt, ignorance is the major enemy of our lives and destinies. People get stagnant, oppressed, bound, and sick because of a lack of knowledge concerning spiritual gifts. Spiritual gifts will always make a difference in your life in Christ Jesus.

Hosea 4:6

My people are destroyed for lack of knowledge. Because you have rejected knowledge, I also will reject you from being priest for Me; Because you have forgotten the law of your God, I also will forget your children.

The knowledge of God's Word will deliver you from the wickedness of this world at anytime and anywhere.

The Power of Knowledge

Knowledge is a powerful tool. Through knowledge alone, a generation can get established and preserved from calamity or destruction.

Proverbs 24:3-5

Through wisdom a house is built, And by understanding it is established; By knowledge the rooms are filled With all precious and pleasant riches. A wise man *is* strong, Yes, a man of knowledge increases strength.

I believe what the children of God need today is divine knowledge. All the doctrinal errors that occur in the body of Christ are because of a lack of knowledge. People will believe any kind of erroneous doctrine that comes to town because they lack divine knowledge. Yes, many lives of people have been destroyed by wrong teachings. The number one thing you and I need today is the Holy Spirit generated knowledge.

That is why one of the major assignments of pastors or ministers of the gospel is to feed people or the church with the knowledge of God's Word. Why? Because the knowledge of God's Word heals, saves, delivers, and restores. There is no way the devil can play satanic schemes in your life if you have God's knowledge. Hence, Jesus once said: you shall know the truth (God's Word) and the truth shall set you free.

Jeremiah 3:15

And I will give you pastors according to mine heart, which shall feed you with knowledge and understanding.

Acts 20:28

Take care *and* be on guard for yourselves and for the whole flock over which the Holy Spirit has appointed you as overseers, to shepherd (tend, feed, guide) the church of God which He bought with His own blood.

I remember the day I began embracing God's Word, my life changed levels. The devil will always take advantage of you when you don't know what is written in

God's Word. God's Word is a spiritual container of our greatness and future in Christ Jesus. There is no way we can walk in greatness if we are ignorant of what Jesus Christ did for us on the cross. Of course, we need knowledge to change the course of our lives.

Reigning in Christ Jesus as a child of God begins with divine knowledge. The knowledge of God's Word is your spiritual equipment against all satanic oppression and bondage. If you want to reign over issues of life, Bible knowledge is a must! Bishop David Oyedepo, one of my spiritual mentors, once said, divine knowledge will always put you in command over issues of life. That is a powerful truth, not just an opinion.

John 8:30-32 (AMP)

As He said these things, many believed in Him. So Jesus was saying to the Jews who had believed Him, "If you abide in My word [continually obeying My teachings and living in accordance with them, then] you are truly My disciples. And you will know the truth [regarding salvation], and the truth will set you free [from the penalty of sin]."

There has to be a knowing for you to walk in your freedom. Most of the times, we don't know or understand what God has done in the covenant of redemption. Otherwise, you wouldn't allow any demonic or oppressive situation to dominate you. Besides, if only you knew the love of God at work in your life, you wouldn't let depression take over your life.

Certainly, if you just knew what Jesus did on calvary 2000 years ago, you wouldn't let those suicidal thoughts take over your life. If you just knew how many angels are surrounding you today, you wouldn't be in bondage to fear. Also, if you just knew how much the Holy Spirit has raised the standard against the devil in your life for your dominion, you wouldn't live in defeat. I pray God opens up your spiritual eyes to see.

Psalm 34:7 (AMP)

The angel of the Lord encamps around those who fear Him [with awe-inspired reverence and worship Him with obedience], And He rescues [each of] them.

Psalm 82:4-5

Deliver the poor and needy; Free *them* from the hand of the wicked. They do not know, nor do they understand. They walk about in darkness; All the foundations of the earth are unstable.

Lacking the divine knowledge of God's Word can crush your destiny in no time. There is no way you can enjoy life in God if you don't even have the basic knowledge of your covenant rights in Christ Jesus. You don't also want to become a burden to anyone, but a blessing and an answer. I refuse to be a burden! Hence, I will carry so much the knowledge of God such that I will become a blessing to someone in my lifetime in Christ Jesus.

Genesis 18:18-20 (AMP)

Since Abraham is destined to become a great and mighty nation, and all the nations of the earth will be blessed through him? For I have known (chosen, acknowledged) him [as My own], so that he may teach *and* command his children and [the sons of] his household after him to keep the way of the Lord by doing what is righteous and just, so that the Lord may bring upon Abraham what He has promised him." And the Lord said, "The outcry [of the sin] of Sodom and Gomorrah is indeed great, and their sin is exceedingly grave.

I encourage you to be like Abraham, whom God trusted with knowledge. Don't weary everyone in your city or society due to lack of knowledge. Equip yourself with the knowledge of God's Word in every department of your life.

Ecclesiastes 10:15

The labor of fools wearies them, For they do not even know how to go to the city!

I pray you become someone's answer in Christ Jesus through the knowledge of God's Word.

Knowledge vs Spiritual Gifts

1 Corinthians 12:1

Now concerning spiritual *gifts,* brethren, I do not want you to be ignorant.

Apostle Paul, by the Spirit of God, refused to be ignorant concerning spiritual gifts.

Ignorance results from a lack of the knowledge of God's Word. When you lack knowledge in any area, you become a victim of life and destiny. Some years ago, I watched a video where a pastor directed his church members to eat grass in order to walk in divine blessings. I believe God that was not biblical, but carnality at its highest level.

Galatians 3:9 (AMP)

So then those who are people of faith [whether Jew or Gentile] are blessed *and* favored by God [and declared free of the guilt of sin and its penalty, and placed in right standing with Him] along with Abraham, the believer.

It is sad to have a pastor lead you to eat grass in order to get closer to God. Sorry; you don't need to eat grass in order to walk in your deliverance. No! Of course, God can direct you to do something unusual, but it should not be a pattern. Then, the same pastor forced his members to drink petrol. When you lack God's Word, you become a victim of bondage. None of all those things will ever bring you closer to God.

Now, why do you think these people did what their pastor ordered them? I believe they lacked the knowledge of God's Word in Christ Jesus. With God's knowledge, you can preserve your life and destiny from trouble. People who follow everything, even what is not in the Word of God, lack knowledge. To be safe in life, you need sufficient knowledge. I will follow nothing in my life but the Word of God only.

We need God's divine knowledge in dealing with spiritual gifts. Especially in these last days, where counterfeit spirits get unleashed to imitate the genuine gifts of the Holy Spirit. One day, I visited a huge marketplace in the centre of Sydney. As I was walking, I just heard someone calling out to me. The man who called me was an Asian by ethnicity. It was fascinating because I did not recognize him in any ways.

Well, when I stopped; he started giving me prophetic words about the next two months of my life. What he said sounded good—but came not from God. Then, as he continued talking to me, he asked me for some money because of giving me those prophetic words. I told him I wasn't interested in what he said—it was false, using the spirit of divination!

Yes, I just knew it in my spirit that he was using demonic influence to convey that message to me about my future. I, in fact, asked him to stop what he was doing, giving false messages to people. Instead, I invited him to give his life to Jesus. Sadly, he ran away in terror. Why? I have adequate knowledge concerning spiritual gifts from

God's Word. That is why those demons in that man could not stand me.

I won't allow any person to come and prophesy over me what is not in line with God's Word. Many people, even Christians, have received wrong and fake prophecies without refuting them. Any false prophetic word that you allow becomes the entry point of demonic activities in your life. Do not accept false prophetic words so that you can please any man or woman of God. You don't have to subscribe to every prophetic word you receive. No!

Sad to say, many innocent people have received false prophetic words without examining them. If you give me a prophecy that by tomorrow morning, I will receive a cheque to the amount of AUD $200, 000 and it doesn't come to pass. Don't say I did not have faith! Sometimes, a prophet can speak presumptuously or with no witness from the Holy Spirit—just the flesh at work. Just be careful in your life.

I believe anything the Holy Spirit speaks will certainly come to pass without struggle. I pray you will have a discerning spirit to know what is from God or not. In the last days, we will see the operation of deceiving spirits in larger numbers. Many people will come in the name of the Lord to seduce many lives of people. Hence, you and I have to be very careful of whom we listen to. God's Word must be number one in our lives.

Deuteronomy 18:21-22

And if you say in your heart, 'How shall we know the word which the Lord has not spoken?'– when a prophet speaks in the name of the Lord, if the thing does not happen or come to pass, that *is* the thing which the Lord has not spoken; the prophet has spoken it presumptuously; you shall not be afraid of him.

Do not be afraid to examine prophecy. It is your covenant right to judge prophecy. Otherwise, unfulfilled prophecy will affect your life if you don't deal with it. It is like giving false hope which does not come to pass (Proverbs 13:12). Hope deferred makes the heart sick! Make sure you write, examine, and follow up on any prophetic word that is given to you.

1 Corinthians 14: 28-30 (AMP)

But if there is no one to interpret, the one [who wishes to speak in a tongue] must keep silent in church; let him speak to himself and to God. Let two or three prophets speak [as inspired by the Holy Spirit], while the rest pay attention *and* weigh carefully what is said. But if an inspired revelation is made to another who is seated, then the first one must be silent.

However, never despise prophecy!

1 Thessalonians 5:20-21 (AMP)

Do not scorn *or* reject gifts of prophecy *or* prophecies [spoken revelations—words of instruction or exhortation or warning]. But test all things carefully [so you can recognize what is good]. Hold firmly to that which is good.

I believe not every prophet is fake. There are so many prophets, apostles, pastors, evangelist and teachers of God's Word who are genuine today. So you can't just criticize or despise everyone you see. No!

CHAPTER 4

Concerning Spiritual Gifts

There are diversities of gifts, but the same Spirit. There are differences of ministries, but the same Lord. And there are diversities of activities, but it is the same God who works all in all. But the manifestation of the Spirit is given to each one for the profit *of all.*

1 Corinthians 12:4-7

Nine Spiritual Gifts

Now, before we discuss the nine spiritual gifts mentioned in 1 Corinthians 9:8-10, I would love you to understand that these gifts are manifestations of the Holy Spirit. They manifest from time to time as the Holy Spirit moves and sees fit. You can't just stand and turn them on and off as you will. No! It is the Holy Spirit who operates them as He wills.

> **1 Corinthians 12:11**
>
> **But one and the same Spirit works all these things, distributing to each one individually as He wills.**

I also want you to know that every child of God has the right to operate in these nine gifts. Of course, the first qualification is that you have to be born again, and the rest follows. Besides, these gifts will operate with more prevalence in those people who need them for spiritual service or ministry. People think these gifts will just manifest anyhow and anywhere. Well, there has to be a reason that glorifies God for them to manifest.

For example, you discover a prophet will have the manifestation of the gift of the word of knowledge more than anyone else. Why? This is because his calling or office needs that gift to function. However, many times, the operations of the spiritual gifts get misused. You don't prophesy just because you want to. No! The Holy Spirit has to come upon you as He sees fit for you to operate in any of the spiritual gifts.

Then, another thing we need to watch out for with spiritual gifts is extremism. Sometimes, those people who operate in these gifts as the Holy Spirit wills forget that these are manifestation gifts. Instead, they want to operate in them even when the Holy Spirit has not moved. They want to turn them on and off without the Holy Spirit operating. In most cases, they step in the flesh—with no anointing—God forbid!

If you try to operate the gifts of the Holy Spirit in the flesh, you will ruin lives and destinies of people. If the Holy Spirit is not moving, do nothing. At least there is one thing you can do, and that is to preach or teach the Word of God. You will never go wrong if you stick with God's Word. What are you trying to prove or achieve? If the Holy Spirit is not moving, do not operate in any gift of the Holy Spirit by yourself—it is dangerous!

Many years ago, I read a book by Kenneth E. Hagin where he shared how a Christian entrepreneur lost his entire fortune in one switch. He got given a false prophetic word concerning his business, and he lost it all. God forbid! Nowadays, Christians are running from one meeting to another, looking for prophetic words. There is nothing wrong with that, but just be careful that no one gives you a word that is not generated by the Holy Spirit.

Apart from that, I have heard of marriages that ended up in divorce because of wrong prophetic words. Each time a prophetic word comes, and is not Holy Spirit guided, it has the potential to destroy lives and destinies of people. Many people have received prophetic words that took them away from God. They are now divorced, and their lives are messed up! I pray to God that will not be your portion in Jesus' name.

1 Corinthians 12:8-10

For to one is given the word of wisdom through the Spirit, to another the word of knowledge through the same Spirit, to another faith by the same Spirit, to another gifts of healings by the same Spirit, to another the working of miracles, to another prophecy, to another discerning of spirits, to

> another *different* kinds of tongues, to another the interpretation of tongues.

In the Scripture above, there are nine spiritual gifts listed. We are going to divide these gifts into three categories for easier understanding.

1) **Revelation gifts**—because they reveal something.
2. **Power gifts**—because they do something.
3. **Utterance gifts**—because they say something.

1. Revelation Gifts

(i) WORD OF WISDOM

> **1 Corinthians 12:8**
>
> For to one is given the word of wisdom through the Spirit...

The word of wisdom is a supernatural ability that is endowed upon someone to give them a solution to a dilemma. The word of wisdom can point out what needs to be done or what will happen in the future. I remember one day I needed to do something in my life, but I got stuck. Then, as I waited upon the Lord in prayer, the word of wisdom came and showed me what to do. I eventually got out of that dilemma without panic.

The word of wisdom implies that from all that God knows, He only gives you a word of His wisdom in order to solve your dilemma. Most of the times, the word of wisdom is in operation, but people don't even know it. However, this wisdom will be more prevalent in the prophetic office and other more ministry gifts.

Apart from that, when a prophet gives a word of knowledge, it will take the word of wisdom to help you know what to do next. Nowadays, we see little of the word of wisdom in operation as compared to the word of knowledge. The only prevalent thing we see in prophets is the word of knowledge. I believe we need all the nine gifts in operation in our lives or churches.

(ii) WORD OF KNOWLEDGE

1 Corinthians 12:8

...to another the <u>word of knowledge</u> through the same Spirit

The word of knowledge is a supernatural gift distributed by the Holy Spirit to anyone He wills or finds. This gift is prevalent in the prophetic office. It is a gift where the Holy Spirit reveals or gives you knowledge of places or events or names of people that you won't know in the natural. The word of knowledge only happens when there is a need, as the Holy Spirit wills.

For example, many years ago, 1996, I went to attend an all night prayer meeting at somebody's house. We prayed that night from 9:00pm up till 6:00am in the morning and God was with us. Now, while praying, I saw a vision of my bedroom and wooden box where I put all my spiritual books. Suddenly, I also saw the very box burning. After that, I saw my elder brother came into the room to put out the fire.

Without doubt, that was the gift of the word of knowledge in operation—there was no way I could have known in the natural. Then, in the morning when I went back home, I found out that one side of the top lid of my wooden box got slightly burnt, however my brother had put the fire out. It was powerful and very encouraging.

Now, as soon as my brother saw me, he exclaimed and said you could have set the entire room and house on fire. Of course, I remember having had left a candle on top of the wooden box. The word of knowledge will always preserve your life and destiny from destruction. Thank God my books and our house got preserved from getting burnt.

Spiritual gifts are vital to the life of a Christian in every way.

All spiritual gifts are there to preserve people's lives and destinies. Sometimes God will let you see things in the future by the word of knowledge. However, it is not something that you orchestrate, but as the Holy Spirit wills. There are many occasions in the Bible where we see the operation of this gift as the Holy Spirit willed. You can't turn them on and off—it is as the Holy Spirit wills.

John 1:47-50

> Jesus saw Nathanael coming toward Him, and said of him, "Behold, an Israelite indeed, in whom is no deceit!" Nathanael said to Him, "How do You know me?" Jesus answered and said to him, "Before Philip called you, when you were under the fig tree, I saw you." Nathanael answered and said to Him, "Rabbi, You are the Son of God! You are the

King of Israel!" Jesus answered and said to him, "Because I said to you, 'I saw you under the fig tree,' do you believe? You will see greater things than these."

Jesus was in a different city, yet He saw Philip sat under a fig tree by the word of knowledge. Just by the word of knowledge, Philip's faith got lit—it was no longer the same. We need spirituals gift in Christ Jesus as never.

(iii) DISCERNING OF SPIRITS

1 Corinthians 12:10

...to another <u>discerning of spirits</u>...

Now, just by the word discerning, you can tell it has a lot to do with knowing or seeing. Discerning of spirits is a supernatural endowment from God by the Holy Spirit to discern spirits—to see and hear in the spirit realm. It has nothing to do with discerning people. Many prophets have missed this nugget, instead they discern people.

Discerning people makes the gift judgmental. Sorry to say, we don't discern human beings or people—but we discern spirits behind the operations. Besides, discerning of spirits is not only limited to evil or demonic spirits. No! You can as well discern angels by this gift as the Holy Spirit wills. Not only that, you can as well discern the spirits of infirmities, sickness, witchcraft, pride, fear, death and much more.

The discerning of spirits enables you to hear and see in the realm of the spirit. We already know that the prophetic office comprises majorly of the gifts of knowing and seeing in the spirit realm. When this gift is in operation by the Holy Spirit, you will get to know exactly what people are going through. However, all operations of spiritual gifts have to be in line with the holy written Word of God. Not what you feel or think!

There are certain times in meetings where you don't know what a person is going through, then suddenly you hear or see in the spirit what is causing the problem. Sometimes, you could sense demons or evil spirits! However, you can't ascribe every problem people are going through today to demonic influence or activity. You need the spirit of discernment to do so.

Sometimes you won't know what is causing sickness or disease in someone's life. Some diseases are because of the presence of demons and others not, but for you to know the cause, it has to be by the discerning of spirits. The other thing is that every child of God, to some extent, can have discernment because of the Holy Spirit. However, the one we are talking about here is a spiritual gift. It only manifests as the Holy Spirit wills.

A good example of discerning of spirits is when Paul the Apostle cast a demon out of a slave girl. The girl operated a business of divination. She made a living out of the spirit of divination or familiar spirits—foretelling the future. In fact, divination is the spirit of witchcraft at work in the life of a person doing it.

Acts 16:16-18

Now it happened, as we went to prayer, that a certain slave girl possessed with a spirit of divination met us, who brought her masters much profit by fortune-telling. This girl followed Paul and us, and cried out, saying, "These men are the servants of the Most High God, who proclaim to us the way of salvation." And this she did for many days.

Had it not been for the gift of discerning of spirits, Paul wouldn't have known that the girl was using the spirit of divination. In fact, the girl spoke wonderful things about Paul, except that she was under the influence of the spirit of divination. Well, as soon as Paul knew, he cast out the demon out of her in the name of Jesus. Hence, I believe the Holy Spirit is not behind everything you hear people say or prophesy.

Another thing is that the slave girl did that for many days without Paul knowing. That shows you and me we don't know everything, only what the Holy Spirit reveals to us. Paul did not operate in that spiritual gift twenty-four hours or all the time. No! It was as the Holy Spirit gave him grace to walk in discernment of spirits. Many people today, even prophets, claim to know everything — no, it has to be by the Holy Spirit—nothing else!

Acts 16:18-19

And this she did for many days. But Paul, greatly annoyed, turned and said to the spirit, "I command you in the name of Jesus Christ to come out of her." And he came out that very hour.

In addition, the young slave girl did divination for many days. Did Paul the Apostle know? No! It was not until the manifestation of the gift of discerning of spirits came forth. All spiritual gifts do not have a remote control that you can turn on and off any time you want to. It is as the Holy Spirit wills. When you prophesy or give a word of knowledge without the Holy Spirit, you can destroy the lives of people. Don't even try it!

(2). Power Gifts

(i) GIFT OF FAITH

> **1 Corinthians 12:9**
>
> ...to another <u>faith</u> by the same Spirit...

Faith is faith! The only difference between the gift of faith and the one mentioned in Romans 10:17 is in manifestation. One comes by hearing and hearing by the Word of God, while the other one comes by the manifestation of the Holy Spirit as a gift.

Like other spiritual gifts mentioned earlier, the gift of faith manifests as the Holy Sprit wills. It is not something that you will always have or possess. No!

The gift of faith is one gift that is needed in order to raise the dead. Hence, there is no ministry established specifically to raise the dead? Why? It all happens as the Holy Spirit wills—not as we wish or plan. That is why you don't just go into hospitals with the common faith and say I will raise everyone from the dead. Yes, don't make that mistake—the Holy Spirit has to manifest the gift of faith to raise the dead.

Above all things, you need this kind of faith in manifestation in your life. This kind of faith is extraordinary and supernatural. You can even tell that it has nothing to do with you. It is like a surging force for supernatural happenings—it does wonders! This faith does not know defeat or giving up—it is Holy Spirit generated faith. Besides, it does not know failure, limitation, complaining, misfortune or stagnation.

I have seen this gift of faith operate in my own life from time to time. It is such a surging faith that puts an end to impossible situations. Assuredly, it has no room for doubt or unbelief—it is a peculiar dimension of faith. We need this kind of faith today for impossible circumstances. I pray you desire this kind of faith or spiritual gift. The gift of faith will bring a unique move of God in the body of Christ Jesus once it gets provoked by our spiritual hunger.

I remember, in the year 2007, I was supposed to graduate from Bible College, but the situation was so bad that it was not possible for me to graduate. There was one subject missing which my college lecturer did not mark. As a result, they did not have the results for me to graduate — what a dilemma! It was terrible and beyond comprehension.

The deadline for the college to have submitted the results to the Department of Education for issuing accredited certificates was on a Friday. Now, it was already Friday evening — there was no hope of graduating at all. I did not know what to do! That meant I had to repeat that subject the following year in order to graduate — spending one more unnecessary year.

Unfortunately, I did not have the time to repeat the subject. It was such a huge stumbling block and a heavy burden to bear. Of course, I had faith, but I needed a different type of faith. Well, when I got up to pray that Friday, I suddenly heard the Lord God assuring me of graduating. It was at that point that there was this surging faith within me. I was at peace!

Then, the following morning on Saturday, I received a phone call from one of my lecturers, who marked my papers right there on the phone. In fact, I scored a credit in that subject, Church Planting, and then on Monday I graduated. I received my Advanced Diploma in Ministry. We need the gift of faith in operation in our lives today.

This kind of faith is also what we call *supernatural faith*. It is not just some extra faith you possess. No! It is a faith that manifests beyond what we can believe God for—it is a spiritual gift of faith. This faith is impulsive—beyond control and understanding. I believe the faith that opened the Red Sea was not common faith, but supernatural faith. God manifested that faith in Moses and the Red Sea opened up.

Hebrews 11:29

By faith they passed through the Red Sea as by dry *land, whereas* the Egyptians, attempting to do so, were drowned.

Supernatural faith in the life of a believer will always triumph in Christ Jesus.

(ii) GIFTS OF HEALINGS

1 Corinthians 12:9

...to another <u>gifts of healings</u> by the same Spirit...

The gifts of healings is another spiritual gift that falls under the "power gifts." Why? This is because this gift does something — it is a doing gift! It is also important to understand that you can't possess this kind of gift every single day. What that means is that it is not a gift that you have for 24 hours of every day. No! It manifests as the Holy Spirit wills and leads you. I pray people understand this truth without prejudice.

I know men and women of God who operate in the healing grace of God regularly with amazing healings. However, this one is different — it only manifests from time to time as the Holy Spirit wills. The moment that happens, there are unusual healings in people's lives. For example, the apostle of faith Smith Wigglesworth operated in this gift most often. Hence, he had so many unusual miracles in his life and ministry.

Now, the Bible does not say gift of healing (singular), but it says gifts of healings (plural). Which means when the gifts of healings manifest, there are diverse operations and healings. When this gift is in manifestation, it does the unbelievable. I have seen this gift operate in my life before. However, it does not just manifest anyhow and anywhere. There has to be a need, and the Holy Spirit has to be in charge.

Yes, healings by the gifts of healings are of another order—they are powerful! In the same way, healings by faith in Christ Jesus and His Word are as powerful. Each time the Holy Spirit manifests His presence or glory, supernatural things happen—healings of all kinds beyond measure. Are you ready for this dimension?

For example, many times the Lord uses me in the healing grace. So when I'm praying for sick people, there are healings that happen because of my faith in the Word of God. While other healings happen when the anointing comes upon me. Yet the more other healings happen when the spiritual gift of healing is in manifestation in my life, as the Holy Spirit wills. All these are operations of the Holy Spirit.

No one will ever engineer the operation of these gifts. It is as the Holy Spirit wills. You don't control them, all you do is yield to the Holy Spirit and then He does everything. One important thing to know is that if this gift is not in manifestation, don't rush to do anything, instead just minister the Word of

God and let people receive healing by faith. You will still get the same results as by the gifts of healings.

(iii) WORKING OF MIRACLES

1 Corinthians 12:10

...to another <u>the working of miracles</u>...

The working of miracles mentioned here are special miracles. However, every miracle is special because they get performed by our Lord Jesus Christ. When we talk of special miracles, we are probably referring to the unusual power behind the miracles. Did you know Jesus is the one who wrought miracles, while the Holy Spirit is the one who operates them as He wills? They all work together as they coexist.

Acts 19:11-12

Now God worked unusual miracles by the hands of Paul, so that even handkerchiefs or aprons were brought from his body to the sick, and the diseases left them and the evil spirits went out of them.

The miracles God did at the hands of Paul were so many and strange. I believe every one of us has seen diverse miracles before, but with every miracle, you could tell that some of them are strange. It is not just a matter of faith—but something beyond your faith — the gift of miracles! The Holy Spirit operates them as He wills, and you can't replicate them at all.

Many years ago, I watched one great man of God with a huge miracle and healing ministry based in the USA. This time, he was holding a healing conference in South America. Now, during one of his meetings, there was a young girl who Jesus healed of a hearing problem. I believe the healing itself was a miracle because of the operation and power behind the healing. It was an unusual working of the Holy Spirit.

In that meeting of the man of God, there was a young girl who was born with one ear missing. She did not have an ear sticking out—it was just skin throughout the ear part. So, when she got healed, she could hear through the skin—that was a special miracle! I believe the healing was not just a healing, but a miracle. When the gift of working of miracles is at work, unusual miracles happen without measure.

Now, as servants of God, we don't know at all times what God intends to do in every meeting. The only thing we do is to believe His Word. In the same way, we don't even know what miracles or healings God wants to perform by His Spirit. All we do and know is that by faith, God will reveal His glory through spiritual gifts by the Holy Spirit. I pray you will see more of the gift of miracles in your life, in Jesus' name.

(3). Utterance Gifts

(i) PROPHECY

1 Corinthians 12:10

…to another <u>prophecy.</u>

What is prophecy? It is an inspired, supernatural utterance of the moment endowed by the Holy Spirit. Prophecy is what you say! There is what we call a "simple gift of prophecy," which every child of God is born to do. There are no restrictions! The simple gift of prophecy is not only for prophets, pastors or those in ministry. No! Anyone born of God—born of the Spirit of God can prophesy as enabled by God.

1 Corinthians 14:1

Pursue love, and desire spiritual *gifts*, but especially that you may prophesy

Prophecy is a divine message from God about the future or what will happen. It is also a message to people about what is in the mind of God. You don't need a special gift to prophesy, all you need is the Holy Spirit in your life. The simple gift of prophecy is for edification—to edify the body of Christ Jesus. How long you have been a Christian has nothing to do with it, but has everything to do with the Holy Spirit.

Prophecy does not need any interpretation at all. It is an obvious message under the inspiration of the Holy Spirit. For example, when I just got born again, I attended a wonderful Pentecostal Church in town. In that church, was an amazing brother who used to prophesy with a simple gift of prophecy. During some meetings, he would stand up and prophesy, accompanied by a strange presence of God.

Apart from that, the presence of God was accompanied by silence, peace, and spiritual edification in the lives of people. Yes, each time the utterance came forth, it was a divine message from God, either for the entire Church or for individuals. Sometimes, His message would come to warn people, to turn away from sin. It was very edifying in every way! I believe all spiritual gifts of God are for our profit in Christ Jesus.

1 Corinthians 12:7

But the manifestation of the Spirit is given to each one for the profit *of all*.

(ii) DIVERSE TONGUES

1 Corinthians 12:10

…to another *different* kinds of tongues

Different kinds of tongues, also known as "diverse tongues," are basically a supernatural utterance in an unknown tongue or language, as the Holy Spirit wills. It is an utterance that has a message from God through human vessels. It is an inspired utterance of the moment to reveal God's mind. The only thing we do is to yield to the Holy Spirit: spirit, soul, and mind. Then we can tap into that realm of divine tongues.

Now, what is the difference between diverse tongues mentioned in 1 Corinthians 12: 10 and the ones in Acts 2:1-13. The difference is that the ones in Acts 2:1-13 are unknown tongues that we speak after the baptism of the Holy Spirit—they are for personal edification. This happened on the day of Pentecost!

Acts 2:1-4

When the Day of Pentecost had fully come, they were all with one accord in one place. And suddenly there came a sound from heaven, as of a rushing mighty wind, and it filled the whole house where they were sitting. Then there appeared to them divided tongues, as of fire, and *one* sat upon each of them. And they were all filled with the Holy Spirit and began to speak with other tongues, as the Spirit gave them utterance.

The "unknown tongues" mentioned in the above Scripture are for spiritual edification and empowerment. Sometimes, the Holy Spirit may give you an interpretation. However, these tongues are much more for personal edification—communicating divine mysteries to God. Speaking in other tongues is a special way to fellowship with God in a divine way. Not only that, it is also the best way to pray according to the will of God.

1 Corinthians 14:2

For he who speaks in a tongue does not speak to men but to God, for no one understands *him;* however, in the spirit he speaks mysteries.

Ever since I got baptised in the Holy Spirit, in 1991, my life has never been the same. I have experienced spiritual edification and growth just by praying in unknown tongues mentioned in Acts 2:1-4. Then, what about the diverse kinds of tongues mentioned in 1 Corinthians 12:10? Well, you can't engineer or orchestrate those—it is as the Holy Spirit wills. These are tongues as a result of the spiritual gift of tongues.

Many years ago, while praying in my prayer room, there was this strange gift of tongues that came upon me. Then, as I kept on speaking these tongues, there was an interpretation that came forth in a known language that I could understand by myself. Do I always have those tongues in my life or meetings? No! Why? That is because all spiritual gifts are manifestations of the Holy Spirit as He wills—not as we will!

1 Corinthians 12:4-6,11

There are diversities of gifts, but the same Spirit. There are differences of ministries, but the same Lord. And there are diversities of activities, but it is the same God who works all in all. But one and the same Spirit works all these things, distributing to each one individually as He wills.

All spiritual gifts are designed to edify the saints and build up the body of Christ Jesus.

(iii) INTERPRETATION OF TONGUES

1 Corinthians 12:10

…to another <u>the interpretation of tongues</u>.

This is also a spiritual gift—it operates and manifests as the Holy Spirit wills. The only tongues you don't need any interpretations for are the ones for personal edification (1 Corinthians 14:2 and Acts 2:1-4). However, when the tongues as a gift (mentioned in 1 Corinthians 12:10) come, they will always need interpretation—especially in a gathering or meeting.

Sometimes you may not have an interpretation. It is as the Holy Spirit wills! However, most of the times when that tongue manifests as a spiritual gift in a meeting, there will always be someone to interpret so that it becomes an obvious message or prophecy to the gatherers or people. That is the Bible way! The Holy Spirit orchestrates all these operations. The only thing we need to do is to cooperate with Him.

Every spiritual gift, if handled well with maturity, will always glorify Jesus. It will always bring glory to God and the lives of people get liberated from bondage. The only secret to every gift is to allow the Holy Spirit to have total pre-eminence. Each time you refuse or ignore to give the Holy Spirit room in your life, that is your downfall. That is why Paul the Apostle asked for spiritual order in handling the spiritual gifts of God.

1 Corinthians 14:27-28

If anyone speaks in a tongue, *let there be* two or at the most three, *each* in turn, and let one interpret. But if there is no interpreter, let him keep silent in church, and let him speak to himself and to God.

1 Corinthians 14:12

Even so you, since you are zealous for spiritual *gifts, let it be* for the edification of the church *that* you seek to excel.

Sometimes, when I'm praying in other tongues, God will give me an interpretation. Does it happen at all times? No! It is as the Holy Spirit wills. Every gift is at the direction and operation of the Holy Spirit. I believe there is no any ironclad rule to it — it is as the Holy Spirit leads, operates, and wills.

In conclusion, one thing you have to understand is that speaking in other tongues is for personal edification. You don't need any interpretation, though you may sometimes have one, while diverse tongues most often need an interpretation if it is in a church gathering or meeting. May God bless you!!

CHAPTER 5

The Works of the Holy Spirit

"I still have many things to say to you, but you cannot bear them now. However, when He, the Spirit of truth, has come, He will guide you into all truth; for He will not speak on His own authority, but whatever He hears He will speak; and He will tell you things to come.

John 16:12-14

Inner Transformation

Philippians 1:6

I am convinced *and* confident of this very thing, that He who has begun a good work in you will [continue to] perfect *and* complete it until the day of Christ Jesus [the time of His return].

When we surrender our lives to Jesus, most of us come with all kinds of baggage. We come with all kinds of weaknesses, confusion, hurt, failure, disappointments, lust, and polluted hearts. All these things rob us of our rich fellowship with God. Hence, the Holy Spirit will start working on our lives from the inside. We call that process "Inner transformation." Transformation starts from the inside of you and then reflects on the outside.

All evil in people comes from the heart (Jeremiah 17:9-10). That is why the

Holy Spirit has to cleanse our hearts from within. The degree to which the Holy Spirit transforms you is determined by the level of your surrender to Him. If you are a Christian who has one foot in the Kingdom of God and another in the world, you will delay your inner transformation. Inner transformation determines your spiritual health.

Matthew 15:19-20

For out of the heart proceed evil thoughts, murders, adulteries, fornications, thefts, false witness, blasphemies. These are *the things* which defile a man, but to eat with unwashed hands does not defile a man."

All that stuff in the heart of a man or woman will need the Holy Spirit to be cleansed out. That is exactly the work of the Holy Spirit. Each time people don't know the primary work of the Holy Spirit, they will walk in bondage without knowing. Hence, when nothing is changing in your life, stop and find out the cause. The Holy Spirit is the sanctifying fire of God and is there to help you get transformed.

Once again, the Holy Spirit will purge your life from evil and wickedness in no time. I believe God will never use a person who won't get sanctified by the Holy Spirit. Hence, it is very important for you and me to allow the Holy Spirit to do a work in our lives. We can't keep doing the same things we used to when we were in the world. No! There has to be a transformation from within our lives—we have to exhibit change!

1 Peter 1-2

> Peter, an apostle of Jesus Christ, To the pilgrims of the Dispersion in Pontus, Galatia, Cappadocia, Asia, and Bithynia, elect according to the foreknowledge of God the Father, in sanctification of the Spirit, for obedience

and sprinkling of the blood of Jesus Christ: Grace to you and peace be multiplied.

I have heard many people say God calls and uses the unqualified. Well, that is very true — God will always use even the least—He is the God of everyone. However, before God uses you in any area, the Holy Spirit has to work on your life. Ministry or service to God is so sacred that for you to minister for the Lord, the Holy Spirit has to transform your life. Hence, don't rush—let the Holy Spirit work on your life.

2 Timothy 2:19-22

Nevertheless the solid foundation of God stands, having this seal: "The Lord knows those who are His," and, "Let everyone who names the name of Christ depart from iniquity." But in a great house there are not only vessels of gold and silver, but also of wood and clay, some for honor and some for dis-

honor. Therefore if anyone cleanses himself from the latter, he will be a vessel for honor, sanctified and useful for the Master, prepared for every good work. Flee also youthful lusts; but pursue righteousness, faith, love, peace with those who call on the Lord out of a pure heart.

For the Lord God to use you, you don't have to be flawless. No! However, you need to be cleansed by the Holy Spirit for the establishment of your relationship with God. Many people have left God, even their ministries, after seeing material blessings — that is a lack of inner transformation. The first work the Holy Spirit does in a child of God happens at new birth. Our human spirit gets regenerated into God's nature.

What the Holy Spirit does at new birth experience is powerful. It is like a motor mechanic removing an old engine from a car and replacing it with a brand new one. The Holy Spirit transmits or injects into us the new life of the Lord Jesus Christ. He removes the stony heart and replaces it with the heart of flesh, full of the life of God. That is why we can't take the work of the Holy Spirit at salvation or new birth for granted.

2 Corinthians 5:17

Therefore if anyone is in Christ [that is, grafted in, joined to Him by faith in Him as Savior], *he is* a new creature [reborn and renewed by the Holy Spirit]; the old things [the previous moral and spiritual condition] have passed away. Behold, new things have come [because spiritual awakening brings a new life].

In Christ Jesus, we are all brand new people — we transition from stony hearts to hearts of flesh.

Ezekiel 36:24-26

For I will take you from among the nations, gather you out of all countries, and bring you into your own land. Then I will sprinkle clean water on you, and you shall be clean; I will cleanse you from all your filthiness and from all your idols. I will give you a new heart and put a new spirit within you; I will take the heart of stone out of your flesh and give you a heart of flesh.

If you are born-again just know that it took the Holy Spirit for you to have a new heart. You are now a new creature in Christ Jesus—no matter your flaws. However, there is yet another work the Holy Spirit does on us—it is on our outside! It is very important for you and me to understand the work the Holy Spirit does on our outside. Our outside is as much important as our inside. We can't undermine any of them.

Now, what that means is that whatever the Holy Spirit has done in your life (the inside of you) should reflect on your outside. That is another work of the Holy Spirit, but it has to be in collaboration with you—you have to be willing. The Holy Spirit will not change your outside if you are not willing. If people see you today, will they see Jesus on you? Your God must also be in the way you talk, act, and relate with people.

Matthew 5:14-16 (AMP)

"You are the light of [Christ to] the world. A city set on a hill cannot be hidden; nor does *anyone* light a lamp and put it under a basket, but on a lampstand, and it gives light to all who are in the house. Let your light shine before men in such a way that they may see your good deeds *and* moral excellence, and [recognize and honor and] glorify your Father who is in heaven.

Outer Transformation

Matthew 5:14,16

You are the light of the world. A city that is set on a hill cannot be hidden. Let your light so shine before men, that they may see your good works and glorify your Father in heaven.

It is hypocrisy to have the light of God inside you and never have it on the outside of you. What we receive at salvation by the work of the Holy Spirit is the light inside. The same light must shine inside and outside. That light is Jesus Christ! Hence, it is our responsibility, by the help of the Holy Spirit, to walk in that light. Once that happens, we call that outer transformation—the light outside. Yes, that is the Bible!

Many believers celebrate the light inside while they are walking in darkness. If your attitude or life has not changed outside, then you are walking in darkness. Of course, you may even carry the light of salvation inside you. It is one thing to be born again and another to walk in the light of your salvation. You discover that someone is born again, yet their outward lifestyle has not changed—it does not reflect Jesus.

John 1:3-5

All things were made through Him, and without Him nothing was made that was made. In Him was life, and the life was the light of men. And the light shines in the darkness, and the darkness did not comprehend it.

John 8:12

Then Jesus spoke to them again, saying, "I am the light of the world. He who follows Me shall not walk in darkness, but have the light of life."

Jesus Christ is that Light that comes into our lives to change both our inner and outer lives. If Jesus has come into your life and your ways or lifestyle are not changing, then there is an enormous problem. We can't come to Jesus and still walk in darkness. Then we need to revisit our spiritual foundations in Christ Jesus.

There are people who have received Jesus, yet they cheat, fight, or sleep with someone's wife or husband. If that is the case, they need the Holy Spirit to transform their outer lives as well. Your deeds as a child of God are equally important and they must reflect Jesus. Your ways and the fruit of your doings or salvation are very important.

Jeremiah 17:9-10

The heart *is* deceitful above all *things,* And desperately wicked; Who can know it? I, the Lord, search the heart, *I* test the mind, Even to give every man according to his ways, According to the fruit of his doings.

Friends, once you engage the Holy Spirit in your life, you will see outer transformation. When we talk of outer transformation, we are talking of your life outside as a Christian or child of God. No one sees your inner life or transformation that took place when you gave your life to Jesus. At least, they see it by the outer life you live. Only then can people witness the power of the cross and the Holy Spirit at work in you.

If you used to be a prostitute or thief, and then suddenly you stop, that alone is a big testimony of the work of the Holy Spirit in you. Hence, you can't celebrate your inner transformation without showing the fruit thereof. People will only believe what they see—they can't believe what they don't see. Your lifestyle and testimony can lead people to Jesus or the cross.

Ephesians 4:20-24

But you have not so learned Christ, if indeed you have heard Him and have been taught by Him, as the truth is in Jesus: that you put off, concerning your former conduct, the old man which grows corrupt according to the deceitful lusts, and be renewed in the spirit of your mind, and that you put on the new man which was created according to God, in true righteousness and holiness.

Matthew 7:20

Therefore by their fruits you will know them.

We need the fruit of our inner transformation to be seen in our deeds or lifestyles. If God transformed the life of Paul the Apostle, once a chief sinner—killing Christians, surely, He shall do it in your own life. All you need is to give room to the Holy Spirit to work in your life. The Holy Spirit won't do anything if you don't let Him!! He can only work in our lives to the degree we Him give room. I pray you give room to the Holy Spirit!

Perfecting the Saints

Ephesians 4:11-14

And He Himself gave some *to be* apostles, some prophets, some evangelists, and some pastors and teachers, for the equipping of the saints for the work of ministry, for the edifying of the body of Christ, till we all come to the unity of the faith and of the knowledge of the Son of God, to a perfect man, to the measure of the stature of the fullness of Christ; that we should no longer be children, tossed to and fro and carried about with every wind of doctrine, by the trickery of men, in the cunning craftiness of deceitful plotting.

The gifts mentioned in Ephesians 4:11 are the five-fold ministry gifts which Jesus gave to the Church when He ascended up on high. Now, the one Jesus left in charge of the operations of miracles, healings, signs, wonders, and spiritual gifts is the Holy Spirit. The Holy Spirit is Jesus here on earth today! For example, when we see the sick get healed, or the dead raised, it is Jesus doing it by the Holy Spirit.

Everything the Holy Spirit does is to glorify Jesus. And everything Jesus does is to glorify the Father in Heaven. Hence, if people yielded to the Holy Spirit in humility for everything, their lives wouldn't be the same. Yielding your entire life to the Holy Spirit is the gateway to experiencing the life transforming power of God in Christ Jesus.

Jesus once said to His disciples that it was for their benefit, even ours, that He was going away so that the Holy Spirit could come. The Holy Spirit is already here on earth—what a privilege! He will lead and take you into all the truth. Jesus left everything in the hands of the Holy Spirit here on earth. That is how blessed we are today! Many people don't know that just having the Holy Spirit is a huge blessing to us.

John 16:7 (AMP)

But I tell you the truth, it is to your advantage that I go away; for if I do not go away, the Helper (Comforter, Advocate, Intercessor-Counselor, Strengthener, Standby) will not come to you; but if I go, I will send Him (the Holy Spirit) to you [to be in close fellowship with you].

If today you dedicated your life to the Holy Spirit, you will see how your life will change. Your life will grow and experience supernatural empowerment in Christ Jesus. I have now come to understand why many Christians, even believers, can never mature in Christ Jesus. It is because they have not allowed the Holy Spirit to take over their lives.

> **Ephesians 4:11-12 (KJV)**
>
> And he gave some, apostles; and some, prophets; and some, evangelists; and some, pastors and teachers; For the perfecting of the saints, for the work of the ministry, for the edifying of the body of Christ.

One of the major works of the Holy Spirit, as shown in the above Scripture, is to perfect the saints. The phrase used "perfecting the saints" means *to mature the saints*. To grow them up! No one will ever mature in spiritual matters of God without the Holy Spirit. Anywhere you see a mature man or woman of God, just know it is the Holy Spirit at work. Your spiritual maturity determines your spiritual command.

We need to mature or grow up in the body of Christ Jesus. There are so many casualties resulting from spiritual immaturity. Spiritual growth is not something the Holy Spirit super imposes on you. Instead, it is your own choice! If you want to grow up spiritually, you will always need to take action of growth. You will need to read the Bible, attend church services, pray and fast. Be willing to undergo change and growth.

Apart from that, create an avenue through which the Holy Spirit can work in your life. It is the Holy Spirit's job to mature you, but yours is to create avenues. Don't just fold your arms doing nothing! Many people think that going to church is enough—sorry, it isn't! You need to come to a place where no should remind you of studying God's Word. Create a spiritual hunger or thirst *avenue* for the Holy Spirit to mature you.

There are several reasons growing up your relationship in God is crucial. For example, there are certain things in life you won't compromise to do when your spiritual life is strong or intact. There are some Christians today who have gone back into the world because of spiritual immaturity. Some could not stand the oppression and eventually gave up on God! There are untold benefits to growing up spiritually in Christ Jesus.

Ephesians 4:13-15

Till we all come to the unity of the faith and of the knowledge of the Son of God, to a perfect man, to the measure of the stature of the fullness of Christ; that we should no longer be children, tossed to and fro and carried about with every wind of doctrine, by the trickery of men, in the cunning craftiness of deceitful plotting, but, speaking the truth in love, may grow up in all things into Him who is the head–Christ.

There are unparalleled benefits of growing up spiritually in Christ Jesus. However, you can never grow up in Christ Jesus by yourself using your human energy or strength. You need the Holy Spirit! I pray you will create room in your life for the Holy Spirit.

CHAPTER 6

Getting Filled with the Spirit

When the Day of Pentecost had fully come, they were all with one accord in one place. And suddenly there came a sound from heaven, as of a rushing mighty wind, and it filled the whole house where they were sitting. Then there appeared to them divided tongues, as of fire, and *one* sat upon each of them. And they were all filled with the

Holy Spirit and began to speak with other tongues, as the Spirit gave them utterance.

Acts 2:1-4

The Indwelling of the Spirit

What is the indwelling of the Holy Spirit? It is a moment in life when the Holy Spirit comes to live inside you after receiving Jesus Christ as your personal Lord and Saviour.

1 Corinthians 3:16-17

Do you not know that you are the temple of God and *that* the Spirit of God dwells in you? If anyone defiles the temple of God, God will destroy him. For the temple of God is holy, which *temple* you are.

If you are born again and you have received the life of Jesus, then the Holy Spirit dwells in you. You don't have to pray and fast and do all those things people try to do to receive the Holy Spirit. As soon as

Jesus comes into your life, the Holy Spirit comes into your life, too. You automatically become the temple of God and the Holy Spirit. The Holy Spirit indwells your born-again human spirit in a measure or degree.

Christians carry God and His Spirit, yet often they don't even know it. They carry the Holy Spirit, who furnished the heavens and the earth, yet they don't even know it. If you are born-again just know that it is a tremendous privilege that you carry God and His Spirit. You don't have to feel it, but you have to believe it. Feelings are not enough to describe the Word of God or the things the Holy Spirit has done in your life.

There is no way the Holy Spirit can come to abide in your life if you are not born-again. In the same way, you can't pray for people to receive the indwelling of the Holy Spirit if they are not born-again. The first thing you can do for such people is to pray for them to receive Jesus. The salvation of your soul is a prerequisite to the indwelling of the Holy Spirit. There is nothing you can do about it—it is God's Word.

There are certain prayers people pray which are unscriptural. You can't pray for people to receive the Holy Spirit if they are not born again. However, you can still pray that the Holy Spirit will provide or protect them. Of course, God will answer that prayer based on His eternal mercy and grace for everyone. Sorry to say, with the indwelling of the Holy Spirit, there has to be first a relationship with Jesus Christ.

When Jesus comes into your life, the Holy Spirit comes in also as a mark of ownership. He seals up your life as a sign or token that you belong to God. The indwelling of the Spirit of God in your life is there for your spiritual relationship with God. It is also a sign that you have eternal life — signifying Jesus! The indwelling of the Spirit of God is your assurance that you are a child of God.

Ezekiel 37:13-15

Then you shall know that I *am* the Lord, when I have opened your graves, O My people, and brought you up from your graves. I will put My Spirit in you, and you shall live, and I will place you in your own land. Then you shall know that I, the Lord, have spoken *it* and performed *it,"* says the Lord.' "

Ezekiel 36:27-28

I will put My Spirit within you and cause you to walk in My statutes, and you will keep My judgments and do *them.* Then you shall dwell in the land that I gave to your fathers; you shall be My people, and I will be your God.

Romans 8:16-17 (AMP)

The Spirit Himself testifies *and* confirms together with our spirit [assuring us] that we [believers] are children of God. And if [we are His] children, [then we are His] heirs also: heirs of God and fellow heirs with Christ [sharing His spiritual blessing and inheritance], if indeed we share in His suffering so that we may also share in His glory.

There is no way you can be born again and never know that the Holy Spirit lives in you. It is the Holy Spirit who teaches and leads you into all truth. He solidifies and establishes your spiritual capacity and relationship with God. People keep on looking somewhere else for help when they are in trouble. Well, the indwelling of the Holy Spirit is enough to give you victory and answers in times of difficulty or trouble.

1 John 1:27 (AMP)

As for you, the anointing [the special gift, the preparation] which you received from Him remains [permanently] in you, and you have no need for anyone to teach you. But just as His anointing teaches you [giving you insight through the presence of the Holy Spirit] about all things, and is true and is not a lie, and just as His anointing has taught you, you must remain in Him [being rooted in Him, knit to Him].

I pray you will be conscious of the abiding presence of the Holy Spirit in your life.

Infilling of the Spirit

Acts 2:1-4

When the Day of Pentecost had fully come, they were all with one accord in one place. And suddenly there came a sound from heaven, as of a rushing mighty wind, and it

> filled the whole house where they were sitting. Then there appeared to them divided tongues, as of fire, and *one* sat upon each of them. And they were all filled with the Holy Spirit and began to speak with other tongues, as the Spirit gave them utterance.

What is the infilling of the Holy Spirit? It is a time when you get filled with the Holy Spirit. However, the infilling does not start or stop when someone gets baptized in the Holy Spirit with the evidence of speaking in other tongues. The Holy Spirit baptism is a starting point — and there are more dimensions of the infilling that happen in the life of a believer.

The more inner transformation happens by the Holy Spirit, the more we get filled with the Holy Spirit. We can get filled with the Holy Spirit to an overflowing dimension, where we can walk in liberty in Christ Jesus. Speaking in tongues is a sign of being filled with the Holy Spirit. However, there are more other dimensions to being filled with the Holy Spirit. I pray you don't just end up with speaking in tongues—seek more!

Luke 1:13-16

> But the angel said to him, "Do not be afraid, Zacharias, for your prayer is heard; and your wife Elizabeth will bear you a son, and you shall call his name John. And you will have joy and gladness, and many will rejoice at his birth. For he will be great in the sight of the Lord, and shall drink neither wine nor strong drink. He will also be filled with the Holy Spirit, even from his mother's womb. And he will turn many of the children of Israel to the Lord their God.

John the Baptist got filled with the Spirit of God from his mother's womb. Then, being filled with the Holy Spirit is a continuous divine agenda of God. The Word of God encourages us to getting filled with the Holy Spirit in our lives. It is essential to being filled with the Holy Spirit daily. When Paul the Apostle wrote to the Ephesian believers, he encouraged them not to be drunk with wine, but to be filled with the Holy Spirit.

Ephesians 5:17-21

Therefore do not be unwise, but understand what the will of the Lord *is*. And do not be drunk with wine, in which is dissipation; but be filled with the Spirit, speaking to one another in psalms and hymns and spiritual songs, singing and making melody in your heart to the Lord, giving thanks always for all things to God the Father in the name of our Lord Jesus Christ, submitting to one another in the fear of God.

When you get filled with the Holy Spirit, your life takes a new turn in Christ Jesus. You walk in supernatural empowerment.

There are many people today who are born-again and baptised in the Holy Spirit, yet they walk in the flesh. I have met people who speak in other tongues, yet they struggle with pornography. I believe being baptised in the Spirit does not mean you have arrived—get filled with the Spirit!

When Jesus got baptised in the Jordan river, He went into the wilderness in the fullness of the Spirit of God. Then He came back from the wilderness in the power of the Holy Spirit. Having the indwelling of the Spirit differs from the infilling, and the infilling differs from being filled with the power of God. I have seen many Christians who get filled with the Spirit, yet they walk in zero power. Speaking in tongues does not equal power.

Luke 4:1-2

Then Jesus, being filled with the Holy Spirit, returned from the Jordan and was led by the

> Spirit into the wilderness, being wilderness, being tempted for forty days by the devil. And in those days He ate nothing, and afterward, when they had ended, He was hungry.

In Luke 4:1-2, Jesus got filled with the Holy Spirit and was led into the wilderness to be tempted by the devil for forty days. Then, in Luke 4:14, Jesus returned from the wilderness in the power of the Holy Spirit. Having the indwelling of the Holy Spirit or getting filled with the Holy Spirit is not equal to power. I believe they are two different things. I pray you will move from being filled with the Spirit to being filled with the power of God.

Luke 4:13-14

> Now when the devil had ended every temptation, he departed from Him until an opportune time. Then Jesus returned in the power of the Spirit to Galilee, and news of Him went out through all the surrounding

region. And He taught in their synagogues, being glorified by all.

There was a reason Jesus did not just end up at the point of being filled with the Spirit. Instead, He went up to the point of power. We need the indwelling and infilling of the Holy Spirit, but much more the power of the Spirit. I pray you will desire to walk in the power of the Holy Spirit as never. Jesus, before He left for Heaven, asked His disciples to never leave Jerusalem until they got endued with the power of the Holy Spirit.

Acts 1:7-18

And He said to them, "It is not for you to know times or seasons which the Father has put in His own authority. But you shall receive power when the Holy Spirit has come upon you; and you shall be witnesses to Me in Jerusalem, and in all Judea and Samaria, and to the end of the earth."

Always remember that walking in dominion or victory demands the power of the Holy Spirit.

The Power of the Spirit

Luke 4:14-15

Then Jesus returned in the power of the Spirit to Galilee, and news of Him went out through all the surrounding region. And He taught in their synagogues, being glorified by all.

Once again, Jesus went into the wilderness in the fullness of the Spirit and returned to Galilea in the power of the Holy Spirit. There is something extraordinary about the power of the Holy Spirit. Hence, every child of God needs to be desperate for it. Of course, you may have an indwelling or infilling of the Holy Spirit, yet there is another dimension called *the power of the Spirit.* So which one do you want?

The power dimension of the Spirit will always distinguish you. With this dimension, you will walk on the devil and the works of darkness without struggle. I have been in meetings where people speak in tongues, yet there is no power to match. Why? It is one thing to have the indwelling or infilling of the Holy Spirit and another to walk in the power of the Holy Spirit. Hence, don't mistake grammar for power!

Jesus Christ, our Lord and Saviour, is our role model. We are to walk in His footsteps! God anointed Him with the Holy Spirit and power. In the same way, we need the power of the Holy Spirit in this time and the one to come. Without the power of the Holy Spirit, we can't survive the powers of darkness engineered against us. We need the power of the Holy Spirit in order to fulfill our glorious destinies here on earth.

Acts 10:38

How God anointed Jesus of Nazareth with the Holy Spirit and with power, who went about doing good and healing all who were oppressed by the devil, for God was with Him.

The power of the Holy Spirit does not fall into your laps. You instead go for it! Jesus went into the wilderness for forty days to get it. You may say, "Well, Pastor George, Jesus did it for me—so there is no need for me to go into the wilderness." Well, there is no one sending you into the wilderness! Of course, you need prayer and fasting to grow in the power of the Spirit of God.

    I have done a lot of prayer and fasting in my life and I'm still doing it today. Why? That is because it takes prayer and fasting to grow in the power of the Spirit. Through prayer and fasting, your flesh gets under subjection to your born-again human spirit. Then, it is at that point the Holy Spirit will have more influence over your life. He will transform, empower, reconstruct, and rekindle your entire life with His power.

Psalm 63:1-2

O God, You *are* my God; Early will I seek You; My soul thirsts for You; My flesh longs for You In a dry and thirsty land Where there is no water. So I have looked for You in the sanctuary, To see Your power and Your glory.

I have heard of men and women of God who prayed and fasted so much that God's power came upon them. Then, just entering church meetings, people got healed and delivered. Preaching and talking about the power of the Spirit does not bring it. The thing that brings it is prayer and fasting, coupled with consecration. We can accomplish nothing without God's power in this world. We need God's power!

I don't know about you, but I'm looking forward to walking in higher dimensions of the power of the Spirit. You can't manifest to the world as a son of God without the power of the Spirit in your life. The entire world is looking for the manifestations of the sons of God. However, the sons cannot manifest because they need the power of the Spirit of God. I have walked in some dimensions of power, but I need more!

Romans 8:19-22

For the earnest expectation of the creation eagerly waits for the revealing of the sons of God. For the creation was subjected to futility, not willingly, but because of Him who subjected *it* in hope; because the creation itself also will be delivered from the bondage of corruption into the glorious liberty of the children of God. For we know that the whole creation groans and labors with birth pangs together until now.

I pray you will manifest your sonship status in Christ Jesus. The Kingdom of God is looking for you to walk in the power of the Holy Spirit to liberate the dying world!!

CHAPTER 7

The Fruit of the Holy Spirit

But the fruit of the Spirit is love, joy, peace, longsuffering, kindness, goodness, faithfulness, gentleness, self-control. Against such there is no law. And those *who are* Christ's have crucified the flesh with its passions and desires.

Galatians 5:22-24

Not an Option

The greatness of a man or woman is not so much in the spiritual gifts they have, but in the fruit of the Holy Spirit. If you can walk in the fruit of the Holy Spirit, there is no amount of darkness or wickedness that can stand you. The fruit of the Spirit is vital.

Ephesians 5:8-9

> For you were once darkness, but now *you are* light in the Lord. Walk as children of light (for the fruit of the Spirit *is* in all goodness, righteousness, and truth)

Most often, believers celebrate spiritual and ministry gifts, but very few celebrate the fruits of the Spirit. It is very possible to perform signs, miracles and wonders, but still miss Heaven! It is not a good idea to spend all your life building your spiritual gifts more than the fruit of the Holy Spirit. The fruit of the Holy Spirit will preserve you from falling. I pray we will have more Christians walking in the fruits of the Spirit.

The flesh is the number one enemy of your spiritual life. Hence, you can't talk about spiritual growth or health, and still entertain the flesh. I have seen many people who walk in the power of the gifts of the Spirit, who never lasted in life and ministry. Why? They lacked the fruit of the Holy Spirit to sustain their spiritual gifts. If you want to last long in life and ministry, then build up the fruit of the Spirit in your life.

> But the fruit of the Spirit is love, joy, peace, longsuffering, kindness, goodness, faithfulness, gentleness, self-control. Against such there is no law. And those *who are* Christ's have crucified the flesh with its passions and desires.

In this chapter, we are looking at love as one major fruit of the Holy Spirit. Without doubt, love is the very highway to greatness and victory. It will stand out anywhere you place it. Love will bring you into a rich relationship with the God of signs, miracles, and wonders. I believe love is the greatest treasure in the Kingdom of God.

John 15:34-35

A new commandment I give to you, that you love one another; as I have loved you, that you also love one another. By this all will know that you are My disciples, if you have love for one another."

If God is love, then we must desire to learn more about love as a fruit of the born-again human spirit.

Love is a Powerful Fruit

1 Corinthians 13:11-13

When I was a child, I spoke as a child, I understood as a child, I thought as a child; but when I became a man, I put away childish things. For now we see in a mirror, dimly, but then face to face. Now I know in part, but then I shall know just as I also am known. And now abide faith, hope, love, these three; but the greatest of these *is* love.

Love is the greatest fruit there is in our lives. Everything else shall pass away, but it abides forever. What is love? Love is God! The word love gets derived from a Greek word "agape," which means unconditional or supernatural love. When Jesus comes into our lives, this love gets deposited into our hearts by the Holy Spirit. It is not something we can work for, it is a gift! However, we have the responsibility to grow it!!

Romans 5:5

Now hope does not disappoint, because the love of God has been poured out in our hearts by the Holy Spirit who was given to us.

The power of love can overcome any problem or challenge in this world. Hence, it is an error to determine your spirituality through your spiritual gifts. Instead, you determine your spirituality by your love walk in Christ Jesus. Of course, that is the Bible way! However, many people determine how spiritual they are by their gifts—not by their love walk in Christ Jesus.

When I talk of a love walk, I'm not talking about giving gifts or burning yourself for people. No! Love is none of that! You can pray in the tongues of men or angels, but still have zero love. You can even have strong faith to move mountains, but still have zero love in you. Love is a place where no matter the hurt, you still decide to love the haters. Why? Because you want to obey the commandment of God to love.

Sad to say, many times people have misinterpreted the meaning of God's love, even in churches. Giving a gift to someone is not a proof that you love them. No! People will give you a gift or help you because you look poor or stranded. They will look down on you! You can give without love, but you cannot love without giving. May you not have your giving or faith disqualified because you lack the love of God.

1 Corinthians 13:1-3

Though I speak with the tongues of men and of angels, but have not love, I have become sounding brass or a clanging cymbal. And though I have *the gift of* prophecy, and understand all mysteries and all knowledge, and though I have all faith, so that I could remove mountains, but have not love, I am nothing. And though I bestow all my goods to feed *the poor,* and though I give my body to be burned, but have not love, it profits me nothing.

Love is the greatest fruit there is, and it has a lot to do with the spiritual condition of your life.

Love is the Way to Victory

Why is love the way to victory? It is because love is God and it never fails. It endures forever!

1 John 4:15-16

> Whosoever shall confess that Jesus is the Son of God, God dwelleth in him, and he in God. And we have known and believed the love that God hath to us. God is love; and he that dwelleth in love dwelleth in God, and God in him.

He that dwells in love dwells in God, and God dwells in him/or her. Dwelling in God and God dwelling in you is victory already. Hence, there are certain battles you don't have to pray and fast for in order to overcome them. All you need is for you to walk in the divine love of God in Christ Jesus. In fact, buying your wife a present is not the love I'm talking about here. I'm talking about the God-kind of love motivated by the Word of God.

I believe for every child of God to make it in life needs the God-kind of love known as the "agape." This kind of love will always win battles of life at anytime and anywhere. Often, we talk about love and we don't even know what genuine love is all about. It has nothing to do with your feelings or emotions. Love is not a feeling, it is the commandment of God's Word. We need to have sufficient revelations about the love of God.

Romans 5:5-8

Now hope does not disappoint, because the love of God has been poured out in our

> hearts by the Holy Spirit who was given to us. For when we were still without strength, in due time Christ died for the ungodly. For scarcely for a righteous man will one die; yet perhaps for a good man someone would even dare to die. But God demonstrates His own love toward us, in that while we were still sinners, Christ died for us.

Jesus died for us while we were still sinners — that alone was love at work. In Christ Jesus, love never fails—it will always prevail. Walking in love is walking in God and His presence. Hence, no matter how much faith you have, it will always require love to work. Replacing love with prayer and fasting is ignorance. Of course, victory can respond to prayer and fasting, but much more to your love walk in Christ Jesus.

In one of my books titled "Forgiveness, the Highway to Victory," I shared that there was one man, a pastor who suffered from some sickness for many years. He visited many doctors and pastors for healing, but with no victory. The man was still sick even after being prayed for by healing evangelists. Until one man of God, through the word of knowledge, told him what was hindering his healing—even unforgiveness!

Further, the man of God directed him to go to the prayer room and forgive people he couldn't forgive. Now, as soon as he did that, the healing manifested in his body. Love is the way to victory! Hence, no matter how much you pray, without a love walk, nothing happens — you will still walk in defeat. Most of the defeats people experience today are not even from the devil, but failure to walk in the love of God.

Nothing will ever stop love because love is God and we all know that God is unstoppable. Never hold grudges against anyone in your life—keep a clean and free spirit in God. Apart from that, never choose to walk in the flesh, but choose to walk in the spirit. You may ask, "How am I going to do it, Pastor George?" Well, the Holy Spirit is there to help us—it is not by mighty nor by power. You just need to ask Him in faith!

There are two things that will always please God, and among those two, one is the greatest (1 Corinthians 13:13). Yes, no one can please God without faith and love in Christ Jesus. There is no way you can walk in defeat if you are walking in love. Walking in love towards God and His people will win you favor in the sight of God. Love remains the greatest commandment Jesus came to introduce us to—yes, it is!

Matthew 22:36-40

Teacher, which *is* the great commandment in the law?" Jesus said to him, "'You shall love the Lord your God with all your heart, with all your soul, and with all your mind.' This is *the* first and great commandment. And *the* second *is* like it: 'You shall love your neighbor as yourself.' On these two commandments hang all the Law and the Prophets."

Never repay evil for evil, but good for evil. Love always strives to please God.

Ephesians 4:25-32

Therefore, putting away lying, "*Let* each one *of you* speak truth with his neighbor," for we are members of one another. "Be angry, and do not sin": do not let the sun go down on your wrath, nor give place to the devil. Let him who stole steal no longer, but rather let him labor, working with *his* hands what is good, that he may have something to give him who has need.

Love will give you victory in every place, just embrace it with all of your heart.

Ephesians 4:29-32

Let no corrupt word proceed out of your mouth, but what is good for necessary edification, that it may impart grace to the hearers. And do not grieve the Holy Spirit of God, by whom you were sealed for the day of redemption. Let all bitterness, wrath, anger, clamor, and evil speaking be put away from you, with all malice. And be kind to one another, tender hearted, forgiving one another, even as God in Christ forgave you.

Always remember this! It will always take the Holy Spirit to walk in the love of God. It is not what your mind or flesh can do, but what the Holy Spirit can do. I pray that your life will never be the same in Jesus' name!!

Final Words of Faith

1. The Holy Spirit is God, not a wind, force, breeze, noise, or an object.
2. The Holy Spirit is behind every miracle, sign and wonder we see today.
3. Without the Holy Spirit, it is impossible to live a holy life.
4. The Holy Spirit is here on earth to glorify and reveal the person of Jesus.

5. The Holy Spirit is: Omnipresent—everywhere, Omnipotent—all powerful, Omniscient—knows everything.
6. Jesus lives or dwells in our lives by the Holy Spirit.
7. The Holy Spirit is our holy teacher and comforter.

OTHER BOOKS BY GEORGE MFULA

- The Covenant Force of Righteousness
- Keys to Preserving Your Destiny
- Walking In Financial Dominion
- Unveiling the Hidden Treasures of Redemption
- The Broken & Forgotten Woman
- Understanding the Divine Secrets of God
- The Secret Place
- Nine Pillars of Success
- Winning the Battle Over Fear
- From Prison To Palace
- The Believer's Authority
- Plans, Purposes and Pursuits
- Breaking Satanic Limitations
- The Incredible Power of God's Word
- Following God's Plan for Your Life
- Exploits of Faith

- The Power of Prayer
- Dynamics of Bible Holiness
- Forgiveness

MINISTRY CONTACT DETAILS

Email: riseandwalk@hotmail.com

Phone: +61-425-338-781

For more information

please visit our website:

WWW.RISEANDWALK.ORG.AU

ABOUT THE AUTHOR

GEORGE MFULA is the overseer of Rise & Walk Church, Australia. He is an author, speaker, pastor, leader, teacher and prophet. His mandate is to liberate people from all oppressions of the devil through the preaching and teaching of the Word of faith. His passion is to glorify Jesus and declare him Lord to all nations of the earth through the matchless power of the pure Word of God and the Holy Spirit.

ABOUT THE BOOK

The Holy Spirit, His Presence & Works is written to bring you into great fellowship with Jesus and the Holy Spirit. Now, the Holy Spirit is not a wind, force, breeze, noise, or an object. The Holy Spirit is God and Jesus here on earth. Hence, every miracle, wonder, or healing we see today in church is at the root of the Holy Spirit and His presence.

Neglecting the Holy Spirit, His presence and works, is burying and destroying your own destiny without knowing. No one can even get saved or go to Heaven without the Holy Spirit. In this book, Pastor Mfula delves deeper to expose immeasurable things that the Holy Spirit can do in your life, including His supernatural operations and power.

When someone is struggling spiritually, it is because of poor fellowship with the Holy Spirit. The Holy Spirit will ignite your spiritual life and capacity if you give Him room in your life. Even victory is at the root of the Holy Spirit.

Get this book! Your life will never be the same!!